HUMOR IS

Charlie "Tremendous" Jones

Tremendous

and Bob Phillips

Tyndale House Publishers, Inc.
Wheaton, Illinois

Scripture quotations are from *The Living Bible,* copyright
1971 by Tyndale House Publishers, Inc.

Library of Congress Catalog Card Number 88-50298
ISBN 0-8423-1361-3
Copyright 1988 by Charlie E. Jones and Bob Phillips
Printed in the United States of America

5   6   7   8   9   93 92 91 90

To all the brilliant connoisseurs
of great humor
who have the
outstanding intelligence
to purchase this book

To our wives,
who laugh at their husbands' jokes,
not because the jokes are clever,
but because they are

CONTENTS

This is the
   Introduction. 11
These are the jokes,
   folks. 17

Abdomen. 19
Ability. 19
Accident. 19
Accuse. 19
Aches and pains. 19
Action. 20
Acupuncture. 20
Adaptability. 20
Adolescence. 20
Advice. 20
After-dinner
   speaker. 21
Age. 21
Alimony. 22
Ambition. 22
Analyst. 22
Angels. 22
Anniversary. 22
Anonymous. 22
Antique. 22
Applause. 23
Arsenic. 23
Ashamed. 23
Astronaut. 23
Attention. 23
Attitude. 23
Auctioneer. 23
Average. 24

Baby. 25
Baby-sitter. 25
Bachelor. 25
Bag. 25
Bargain. 25
Beans. 26
Belief. 26
Best years. 26
Bigamy. 26

Birth certificate. 26
Birthstone. 26
Blindness. 26
Blue jeans. 26
Bluff. 26
Blush. 27
Boast. 27
Books. 27
Bore. 27
Borrowing. 27
Boss. 28
Bottom. 28
Brat. 28
Breakdown. 28
Breath. 28
Bridegroom. 28
Brushing. 28
Budget. 28
Burden. 28
Business. 29
Busybody. 29

Cackling. 31
Camelot. 31
Candidates. 31
Cannibal. 31
Catty. 31
Cemetery. 31
Census. 32
Character. 32
Charge. 33
Chase. 33
Chauvinism. 33
Cheap. 33
Check. 34
Checking. 34
Chess. 34
Children. 34
China. 35
Chivalry. 35
Chocolate. 35
Choir. 35
Chop to the ego. 35

Christmas. 35
Church. 36
Church signs. 36
Cigarette. 37
Civilization. 37
Clergyman. 37
Clever. 37
Climbing. 38
Cloverleaf. 38
Coffee. 38
Cold cream. 38
Cold cut. 38
College. 38
College-bred. 39
Colonel Sanders. 39
Comeback. 39
Commercials. 39
Common sense. 39
Commonwealth. 39
Communication. 39
Companions. 39
Conceit. 40
Confidence. 40
Congratulations. 40
Congressmen. 40
Conquer. 40
Conscience. 40
Contented. 40
Conversation. 40
Converted. 41
Conviction. 41
Cookies. 41
Cooks. 41
Corns. 41
Correspondence. 41
Cosmetics. 41
Cost of living. 41
Counselors. 41
Courage. 42
Cowardice. 42
Crabby. 42
Crazy. 42
Criticism. 42
Cupid. 43

Dance. 45
Date. 45
Dead. 45
Deaf. 45
Deaf-mute. 46
Deafness. 46
Deeds. 46
Dentist. 46
Desperation. 46
Dig. 46
Dinner speaker. 46
Discuss. 47
Disobey. 47
Distrust. 47
Doctor. 47
Do-it-yourself. 48
Driving. 48
Drum. 48
Dull. 48
Dumb. 49

Earache. 51
Ecstasy. 51
Egotist. 51
Elbows. 52
Eloquence. 52
Embarrassed. 52
Employment. 52
Endangered. 52
Enemy. 52
Engagement ring.
  52
Err. 53
Escape. 53
Estimate. 53
Etiquette. 53
Evil. 53
Example. 53
Execute. 53
Exercise. 54
Expenses. 54
Explain. 54

Face-lift. 55
Failure. 55
Fainted. 56
Faith. 56
Falling. 56

Familiarity. 56
Fanaticism. 56
Fast. 56
Father. 56
Feeble. 56
Filibuster. 57
Fine. 57
Finish. 57
Fire. 57
Fireproof. 58
Fishing. 58
Flattery. 58
Flee. 58
Flexibility. 58
Flirting. 58
Flooded. 58
Floorwalkers. 58
Food. 59
Football. 59
Forgiveness. 59
Fortune. 59
Frankness. 59
Freedom. 59
Friend. 60
Frustration. 60
Funeral. 60

Gambling. 61
Generosity. 61
Genius. 61
Germs. 61
Girls. 62
Giving. 62
God. 62
Golf. 62
Good old days. 62
Gossip. 63
Grace. 63
Graffiti. 63
Groan. 63
Grouch. 63
Group therapy. 64
Growls. 64
Guilt. 64
Guru. 64

Habit. 65
Hair color. 65

Hanged. 66
Happy. 66
Hat. 66
Heroism. 66
High heels. 66
Hippopotamus. 66
Hobby. 67
Home. 67
Honeymoon. 67
Horn. 67
Horseradish. 67
Horse sense. 67
Horse stealing. 68
Humor. 68
Hypochondriac. 68
Hypocrite. 68

Ideal husband. 69
Ideal wife. 70
Identity crisis. 71
Idiot. 71
Imitation. 71
Independent. 71
Insanity. 71
Insurance. 71
Introduction. 73
IRS. 73
It's a boy. 73

Joke. 75
Judgment. 75
Junk. 75

Kayak. 77
Kissing. 77
Kitchen. 78

Last minute. 79
Late. 79
Law. 79
Laziness. 79
Lead. 79
Learning. 79
Leisure. 79
Letter. 80
License. 80
Linguist. 80
Little things. 80

Lockjaw. 80
Lost. 80
Love. 81

Man of the Year. 83
Marriage. 83
Memories. 85
Mental illness. 85
Middle age. 85
Minister. 85
Miser. 86
Misjudged. 86
Money. 86
Moses. 86
Mother. 86
Mother-in-law. 87
Mouth. 88
Mozart. 88
Mud. 89
Mud packs. 89
Mushrooms. 89

Nag. 91
Narrow escape. 91
Neglect. 91
Nervous. 91
Newlywed. 91
Next. 92
Nodding. 92
Nothing. 92

Obesity. 93
Obey. 93
Oboe. 93
Observant. 93
Oil. 93
Old maid. 93
Operation. 94
Opinion. 94
Optimist. 94
Order. 94
Originality. 94
Overeating. 94
Overpopulation. 94

Pail. 95
Pain in the neck. 95
Palm reader. 95

Pantyhose. 95
Parents. 95
Payment. 96
Peanut butter. 96
Pelts. 96
Perfection. 96
Performer. 96
Perpetual motion. 96
Personal loan. 96
Piano. 97
Pigs. 97
Pinch. 97
Pirate ship. 97
Place. 97
Planning. 98
Pod. 98
Poison. 98
Politicians. 98
Pollution. 98
Polygamy. 98
Popularity. 99
Positive. 99
Pot. 99
Poverty. 99
Prayer. 99
Preachers. 99
Predict. 100
Prejudice. 100
Prescriptions. 100
President. 100
Pretension. 100
Pretty. 100
Pride. 100
Procrastination. 101
Production. 101
Promises. 101
Psychiatrist. 101
Psychopath. 101
Punctual. 101
Purpose. 101

Quiet. 103

Raise. 105
Reading. 105
Reducing. 105
Relatives. 105

Repetition. 106
Reprimand. 106
Reputation. 106
Resort. 106
Responsibility. 106
Ride. 106
Right. 106
Robin Hood. 106
Rubber band. 107
Rule the world. 107

Salesman. 109
Satisfaction. 109
Satisfied. 109
Sawmill. 110
Seafood diet. 110
Selfishness. 110
Sentence. 110
Separation. 110
Sleep. 110
Smart. 110
Smile. 111
Smoke. 111
Snore. 111
Sowing and
  reaping. 111
Space. 111
Speak. 111
Speaking. 111
Speech. 111
Speeding. 112
Storyteller. 112
Success. 112
Sue. 112
Suicide. 112
Sunburn. 112
Sunshine. 112
Surprise. 113
Sweater. 113
Swell. 113

Tact. 115
Talk. 115
Teacher. 115
Teeth. 115
Television. 116
Temptation. 116
Texan. 116

Thumb. 116
Ticket. 116
Tightwad. 116
Time. 117
Tip. 117
Tongue twister. 117
Top this. 117
Treads. 117
Trifles. 118
Trouble. 118
Truth. 118

Ulcers. 119
Undertaker. 119

Vacuum cleaner. 121
Vegetables. 121
Vows. 121

Water bed. 123
Weak. 123

Weight. 123
Whale. 123
Whisper. 123
Word. 123
Work. 123
Writing. 124

Yawn. 125
Youth. 126

Zeal. 127

This is the Introduction.

HUMOR IS TREMENDOUS. It adds sparkle and zest to one's life. It helps us learn to laugh at the world, ourselves, and others. It helps us not take life too seriously.

Humor can be very useful when speaking to groups. It can be a form of entertainment or a method for reducing tension. Ideas and concepts become more memorable when humor is used. Humor helps to clarify important points. Humor can persuade and convince an audience to take action. Humor can lift the audience for a breath of air when the subject is something serious. Humor encourages the audience to accept truth more easily.

This book of humor can be used for personal enjoyment and as a resource for jokes and stories to share with family and friends or as illustrations in speeches and talks. The purpose of this book is to provide good, clean humor that will fit everyone's needs.

Many people have problems with humor. They don't perceive themselves as funny, or they've never had any luck telling jokes. Here are some frequently heard comments or questions about humor, along with our responses.

I just can't remember jokes. I always forget the punch line.

There are two ways to remember jokes. The first is to write down the joke shortly after you hear it. The second is to share the joke with someone shortly after you hear it. Telling the joke will reinforce it in your memory. The old maxim is true: "We only keep what we give away."

I just can't tell jokes.

Telling jokes is like every other activity in life: if you want to be good at it, you have to practice. Start by telling simple one-line jokes or puns. As you gain success, move on to longer jokes and stories.

Does a good joke always get a laugh?

No, it does not. Response varies with the audience, the delivery of the joke, the time of day, and many other factors. Physical factors are important. For example, if the lighting in the room is dim, the audience won't see the twinkle in your eye. And not every joke is appropriate for every audience. Telling a funeral joke to a group in which someone has recently passed away will cause the death of your joke.

What makes a joke funny?

Many times, humor is in the eye of the beholder. Humor can be likened to a magic trick that is performed with words. It involves an obvious untruth or exaggeration, and it contains a surprise or a punch line or an unexpected twist. It is made up of the *setup* and the *payoff*. The payoff is the revelation or punch line that pulls it all together.

What is the difference between a joke and a comedy technique?

A comedy technique involves funny faces, funny voices, funny accents, and funny gestures. For the average joke teller, it is best to avoid comedy technique. It is usually better to be just yourself. Witty is better than wacky. Psychological humor is better than physical humor as a rule. You don't have to be a professional comedian to be funny.

It seems like many jokes have targets. They seem to pick on people or attack them.

This is true. Humor often pokes fun at bosses, government, authority figures, and various groups. The audience doesn't mind if you hit a target—just don't wipe it out. Attacking others is not acceptable or well received. The most effective target of a joke is yourself. That way you won't offend others, and the audience will accept you as a good sport. Picking on yourself also gives you permission to gently pick on others. With regard to ethnic humor, many people become easily offended. To utilize some really funny ethnic jokes, we invented an imaginary neutral country called Smogaria. Just change all of your ethnic jokes to Smogarian jokes and have some fun. No one will be offended.

What is the difference between a funny joke and a funny story?

A funny story is basically an expanded joke. It involves both humor and fiction wrapped together. To tell a funny story effectively, it is good to practice it.

Is it better to tell short stories or long stories?

It is usually better to stay with short stories and one-liners. If they fail, it is not as traumatic. Longer stories build greater expectations. Your punch line needs to be especially strong in a longer story, or the letdown will be great.

What happens when the joke or story fails?
The first thing is to learn to die with dignity by acknowledging the "bomb." The second thing to do is to profit by it. Examine why the joke did not work. Ask yourself:

a. Was the delivery poor?
b. Was it targeted for the wrong audience?
c. Was it a failure to stress the punch line properly and clearly?
d. Was it a failure of timing?
e. Was the pace too fast or too slow?

Telling jokes can be a lot of fun. Or it can be a disaster, like the man who told a joke and everyone booed except one man: he was applauding the booing.

If you would like to guarantee disaster in your joke telling, follow these suggestions:

1. Make sure you forget the punch line; sadists enjoy a letdown.
2. Laugh at your own joke and be sure to jab your audience during the process. Be sure to slap them on the back, too.
3. Tell the same story over if the point is missed. This will assure at least wry smiles.
4. Make sure the story is long enough to lull the dull ones to sleep.
5. Tell the wrong joke to the wrong audience; they'll feel worse than you do.
6. Above all else, don't be yourself, because you know you're not humorous even if you are funny.

If, on the other hand, you would like to have some measure of success in joke telling—ignore the above suggestions.

By the way, we have included quotes and sayings that may not be, strictly speaking, humorous. Some are selections from the Book of Proverbs, others are sayings of famous people, and others are just words of wisdom that we wanted our readers to see. They are not intended to spoil the fun but to remind us that humor has a genuinely serious purpose. They also provide "serious relief" for readers who may fear that they will overdose on humor. Like the jokes and stories in the book, they are here to remind you that life is tremendous, and so is the ability to laugh and to think.

Have fun!

Charlie "Tremendous" Jones and Bob Phillips

These are the jokes, folks.

A is for Anecdote, Amusement, Aching Sides

ABDOMEN
A bowl-shaped cavity containing the organs of indigestion.

ABILITY
The wind and the waves are always on the side of the ablest navigators. EDWARD GIBBON

Executive ability is deciding quickly and getting somebody else to do the work.

ACCIDENT
A place where absence of body is better than presence of mind.

If four out of five accidents happen at home, why do people live there?

ACCUSE
He that accuses all, convicts only one.

ACHES AND PAINS
I've got so many aches and pains that if a new one comes today, it will be at least two weeks before I can worry about it.

ACTION

Think like a man of action and act like a man of thought.

ACUPUNCTURE

Acupuncture is nothing new. Most married men have been getting needled for years.

There must be something to acupuncture—you never see any sick porcupines.

ADAPTABILITY

The weathercock on the church spire, though made of iron, would soon be broken by the storm wind if it did not understand the noble art of turning to every wind.

ADOLESCENCE

A fellow mentioned that his teenage son was developing a cauliflower ear—not from boxing, but from using the phone.

Adolescence is that time of life when children start bringing up their parents.

Adolescence is that time in a boy's life when he notices that a girl notices he is noticing her.

ADVICE

Advice is seldom welcome, and those who need it the most, like it the least. LORD CHESTERFIELD

We give advice by the bucket, but take it by the grain. WILLIAM ALGER

He that gives good advice builds with one hand; he that gives good counsel and example builds with both; but he that gives good admonition and bad example builds with one hand and pulls down with the other. FRANCIS BACON

It's surprising how many persons will unselfishly neglect their own work in order to tell you how to run your affairs.

Though good advice lies deep within a counselor's heart, the wise man will draw it out. PROVERBS 20:5

Young man, consult your father. He is often as old as you are, and sometimes knows as much.

Socrates was a Greek philosopher who went around giving good advice. They poisoned him.

We are never so generous as when giving advice.

Betty: Does your husband ever take advice?
Sue:　Occasionally, when nobody is looking.

AFTER-DINNER SPEAKER
The guy who starts the bull rolling.

AGE
At twenty years of age the will reigns; at thirty the wit; at forty the judgment. BENJAMIN FRANKLIN

The woman who tells her age is either too young to have anything to lose or too old to have anything to gain.

Her age is her own business—and it looks like she's been in business a long time.

At age twenty, we don't care what the world thinks of us. At thirty, we begin to worry what it thinks of us. At fifty, we find it wasn't thinking of us at all.

The judge pounded his gavel for the court to come to order, then turned to the woman in the witness box.
   "The witness will please state her age," he ordered, "after which she will be sworn in."

Never ask a woman her age; ask it of some other woman.

It's surprising how many persons our age are a lot older than we are.

My wife is something. She never lies about her age. She just tells everyone she's as old as I am. Then she lies about my age.

ALIMONY

Many people like to use bank checks personally designed to express individuality. A California man had a set of checks imprinted with a photograph of himself kissing his new young wife—to be used exclusively to send alimony payments to his ex-wife.

AMBITION

Some folks can look so busy doing nothing that they seem indispensable.

You can't hold a man down without staying down with him. BOOKER T. WASHINGTON

ANALYST

The analyst
Is not a joke:
He finds you cracked
And leaves you broke.

ANGELS

God made man a little lower than the angels, and he has been getting a little lower ever since. WILL ROGERS

ANNIVERSARY

"Does your husband ever remember your wedding anniversary?"

"No, so I remind him of it in January and June, and I get two presents."

ANONYMOUS

The name of a joke book writer.

ANTIQUE

Clerk: This is an ancient Roman candlestick.
Buyer: Are you sure you are not trying to fool me? Is it really that old?
Clerk: Old? When they dug it up, it had written on it "300 B.C."

APPLAUSE

Let's have a round of applause for the wonderful job the program committee did in not being able to obtain a speaker.

Robert Montgomery's advice concerning applause: "Enjoy it, but never quite believe it."

ARSENIC

"I want some arsenic for my mother-in-law."
  "Have you got a prescription?
  "No, but here's her picture."

ASHAMED

Live in such a way that you would not be ashamed to sell your parrot to the town gossip. WILL ROGERS

ASTRONAUT

The astronaut was preparing for his moon launch and being interviewed by the press. "How do you feel?" asked one reporter.
  "How would you feel if you were going to the moon in a vehicle with over 150,000 parts and you knew they were all supplied by the lowest bidder?"

ATTENTION

Hold the ear, and the head will follow.

ATTITUDE

A relaxed attitude lengthens a man's life; jealousy rots it away. PROVERBS 14:30

Those who wish to sing always find a song.

AUCTIONEER

The auctioneer interrupted his chanting to announce that someone in the crowd had lost his billfold containing $1,000 and that he was offering a reward of $200 for its return.
  A voice from the rear of the crowd piped up, "I'll bid $210."

AVERAGE

Not doing more than the average is what keeps the average down.

The average American family consists of 4.1 persons. You have one guess as to who constitutes the .1 person.

 **is for Buffoonery, Belly Laugh**

BABY

An alimentary canal with a loud voice at one end and no responsibility at the other.

BABY-SITTER

Someone you employ to watch your television set.

BACHELOR

A man who prefers to cook his own goose.

BAG

Did you hear about the man who asked the bellboy to carry his bag? The bellboy came over and picked up his wife.

BARGAIN

Think twice over a great bargain, and then leave it.

"Utterly worthless!" says the buyer as he haggles over the price. But afterwards he brags about his bargain! PROVERBS 20:14

Good bargains are pickpockets.

BEANS

Husband: Beans again!
Wife: I don't understand it. You liked beans on Monday, Tuesday, and Wednesday, and now all of a sudden you don't like beans.

BELIEF

One person with a belief is equal to a force of ninety-nine who have only interests.

BEST YEARS

Husband: I gave you the best years of my life.
Wife: Those were the best?

BIGAMY

The extreme penalty of bigamy is two mothers-in-law.

BIRTH CERTIFICATE

She keeps asking her husband to show her his birth certificate. She wants proof that he's alive.

BIRTHSTONE

Son: Dad, this magazine article says that my birthstone is the ruby. What is yours?
Father: The grindstone.

BLINDNESS

Joe: He went blind from drinking coffee.
Moe: How did it happen?
Joe: He left his spoon in the cup.

BLUE JEANS

What people used to wear who worked.

BLUFF

Boy: If you refuse to be mine, I'll hurl myself over that five-hundred-foot cliff over there.
Girl: That's a lot of bluff.

BLUSH

Man is the only animal that blushes. Or needs to.
MARK TWAIN

BOAST

Someone who opens his mouth and puts his feats in.

BOOKS

The man who does not read good books has no advantage over the man who can't read them.
MARK TWAIN

The love of books is an infectious sort of thing. Children don't learn it; they catch it.

BORE

A person who has flat feats.

A borc is a person who is me-deep in his conversation.

A bore is someone who persists in holding his own views after we have enlightened him with ours.

Mark Twain was once trapped by a bore who lectured to him about the hereafter: "Do you realize that every time I exhale, some poor soul leaves this world and passes on to the great beyond?"
    "Really? Why don't you try chewing cloves?"

At a formal dinner the hostess, who was seated at the far end of the table from a very famous actress, wrote a note to the actress and had the butler deliver it.
    The actress couldn't read without her glasses, so she asked the man at her left to read it to her. "It says," he began, "'Dear, do me a favor and please don't neglect the man at your left. I know he's a bore, but talk to him.'"

BORROWING

He who borrows sells his freedom.

BOSS

It's easy to tell who the boss is. He's the one who watches the clock during the coffee break.

BOTTOM

It's a good idea to begin at the bottom in everything except in learning to swim.

BRAT

A child who acts like yours but belongs to a neighbor.

BREAKDOWN

The big trouble with success is that the formula is the same as for a nervous breakdown.

BREATH

Husband: This report says that every time I breathe, three Chinese people die.

Wife: That doesn't surprise me. You've got to stop eating so much garlic.

BRIDEGROOM

The proof that a woman can take a joke.

BRUSHING

One thing about getting old is that you can sing in the bathroom while brushing your teeth.

BUDGET

A group of figures that prove you shouldn't have gotten married in the first place.

Teacher: Who can give me a definition of the word *budget*?

Johnnie: A budget is a family quarrel.

Budget: A mathematical confirmation of your suspicion.

BURDEN

A burden that one chooses himself is not felt.

BUSINESS

There are two times in a man's life when he should not speculate: when he can't afford it, and when he can. MARK TWAIN

BUSYBODY

A person who burns the scandal at both ends.

C is for Cackle, Cutups, Clowning, Chuckle, Chortle

CACKLING

If you would have a hen lay, you must bear with her cackling.

CAMELOT

A place where they sell used camels.

CANDIDATES

Candidates are wondering why so few folks contribute to political campaigns. Somebody should tell them we gave at the supermarket.

CANNIBAL

"Tell me," the missionary asked a cannibal, "do you think religion has made any headway here?"

"Yes," answered the native. "Now we eat only fisherman on Fridays."

Cannibal prince: Am I too late for dinner?
Cannibal king: Yes, everybody's eaten.

CATTY

A cat doesn't have nine lives, but catty remarks do.

CEMETERY

You look like a talent scout for a cemetery.

CENSUS

When the Viking explorer Leif Ericson returned from his New World voyage, he found that his name had been dropped from the registry of his hometown. He reported the omission to the chief town official who, deeming it a slight to a distinguished citizen, protested strongly to the district census taker.

"I'm terribly sorry," apologized the census taker in great embarrassment. "I must have taken Leif off my census."

Question: What do they call census takers in Chinatown?

Answer: Chinese checkers.

CHARACTER

Character is what you are in the dark.
DWIGHT L. MOODY

Character is much easier kept than recovered.

Character is not made in a crisis—it is only exhibited.

The proper time to influence the character of a child is about a hundred years before he is born.

Tears on your pillow will never wash out stains on your character.

When wealth is lost, nothing is lost;
When health is lost, something is lost;
When character is lost, all is lost!

Character is a by-product; it is produced in the great manufacture of daily duty.

The measure of a man's real character is what he would do if he knew he would never be found out.

The difficulty with marriage is that we fall in love with a personality, but must live with a character.

CHARGE

There used to be only two classes of people, but now there are three: the Haves, the Have-nots, and the Charge-its.

CHASE

A man always chases a woman until she catches him.

CHAUVINISM

HOW TO TELL A BUSINESSMAN
FROM A BUSINESSWOMAN

A businessman is dynamic; a businesswoman is aggressive.

He is good on details; she is picky.

He loses his temper; she is crabby.

He's a go-getter; she is pushy.

When he's depressed, everyone tiptoes past his office; when she is moody, it must be her time of the month.

He follows through; she doesn't know when to quit.

He's confident; she is stuck-up.

He stands firm; she's hard as nails.

He has the courage of his convictions; she is stubborn.

He is a man of the world; she's been around.

He can handle his liquor; she's a lush.

He isn't afraid to say what he thinks; she's mouthy.

He's human; she's emotional.

He exercises authority diligently; she is power-mad.

He is close-mouthed; she is secretive.

He can make quick decisions; she's impulsive.

He runs a tight ship; she's hard to work for.

CHEAP

The bitterness of poor quality lingers long after the sweetness of cheap price is forgotten.

CHECK

A young college student wrote home to his family: "Dear Mom and Dad: I haven't heard from you in nearly a month. Please send a check so I'll know you're all right."

CHECKING

Bridegroom: My wife and I have a joint checking account.
Best friend: Isn't that hard to keep straight?
Bridegroom: No. I put in the money and she takes it out.

CHESS

A group of chess players had congregated in the lobby of a big New York hotel. Each person tried to outdo the other in tales of his prowess in mastering opponents. After a while, the hotel manager shouted, "Everybody out!"

Asked why, he said, "I can't stand chess nuts boasting in an open foyer."

CHILDREN

It is dangerous to confuse children with angels.

Sam: My daddy has a sword of Washington and a hat of Lincoln.
Bill: My father has an Adam's apple.

Every couple knows how to raise the neighbor's children, so why not have all families swap children?

Children are a comfort in our old age, it is true; and very often children help us reach it faster, too.

Mother: Bobby, last night there were two pieces of cake in the pantry, and now there is only one. How do you explain that?
Bobby: I guess I didn't see the other piece.

Satan keeps school for neglected children.

Father: Why are you always at the bottom of your class?

Dennis: It doesn't make any difference. They teach the same thing at both ends.

The trouble with your children is that when they're not being a lump in your throat, they're being a pain in your neck.

The greatest aid to adult education is children.

CHINA

"What do you think of Red China?" one lady asked another during a luncheon discussion of world affairs.

"Oh, I don't know," replied the other lady. "I guess it would be all right if you used it on a yellow tablecloth."

CHIVALRY

The attitude of a man toward someone else's wife.

CHOCOLATE

My wife is a lousy cook. The first time she made dinner I choked on a bone in the chocolate pudding.

CHOIR

John: What made you give up singing in the choir?

Jack: I was absent one Sunday, and someone asked if the organ had been fixed.

CHOP TO THE EGO

"Whatever I say goes."

"Then why don't you talk about yourself for a while?"

CHRISTMAS

Many a Christmas tie is in a clash by itself. BOB ORBEN

Anyone who thinks Christmas doesn't last all year doesn't have a charge account.

"For Christmas," a woman remarked to her friend, "I was visited by a jolly, bearded fellow with a big bag over his shoulder. My son came home from college with his laundry."

There seems to be some question as to whether more gifts are exchanged on Christmas or the day after.

CHURCH

A place where you encounter nodding acquaintances.

Some go to church to take a walk;
Some go there to laugh and talk;
Some go there to meet a friend;
Some go there their time to spend;
Some go there to meet a lover;
Some go there a fault to cover;
Some go there for speculation;
Some go there for observation;
Some go there to doze and nod;
The wise go there to worship God.

Wife: Did you see that hat Mrs. Jones wore to church?
Husband: No!
Wife: Did you see the new dress Mrs. Smith had on?
Husband: No!
Wife: A lot of good it does you to go to church!

CHURCH SIGNS

Come in and have your faith lifted.
Come in and let us prepare you for your finals.
A miser is a rich pauper.
Ask about our pray-as-you-go plan.
We hold sit-in demonstrations every Sunday.
No matter how much you nurse a grudge, it won't get better.

Start living to beat hell.

If some people lived up to their ideals they would be
  stooping.

Everything you always wanted to know about
  heaven and hell but were afraid to ask.

Pray up in advance.

Patience is the ability to stand something as long as
  it happens to the other fellow.

Think twice before you speak and you may say
  something even more aggravating.

CIGARETTE

A political prisoner was about to be executed by the
new dictatorial regime. He was blindfolded by the
captain of the firing squad and asked if he wanted a
cigarette.

"No, thank you," said the prisoner, "I'm trying to
quit."

CIVILIZATION

After several thousand years, civilization has
progressed to a point where we lock all our doors
and windows every night while jungle natives sleep
in open huts.

CLERGYMAN

Clergyman: I've lost my briefcase.
Traveler: I pity your grief.
Clergyman: I pity the thief.

CLEVER

"Do clever men make good husbands?"
  "Clever men don't become husbands."

"Bill's wife always laughs at his jokes."
  "They must be pretty clever."
  "No—she is."

Find enough clever things to say, and you're a
prime minister; write them down, and you're
Shakespeare. GEORGE BERNARD SHAW

CLIMBING

To keep from falling, keep climbing.

CLOVERLEAF

There is a growing sentiment that the national flower should be concrete cloverleaf.

COFFEE

They serve blended coffee—today's and yesterday's.

COLD CREAM

My wife spends a fortune on cold creams and oils. She puts them all over her body. I went to grab her, but she slid out of the bed.

COLD CUT

Buck: Were you ever married?
Glen: Yeah, but my wife ran away.
Buck: How did it happen?
Glen: She ran away when I was taking a bath.
Buck: I'll bet she waited years for the opportunity.

COLLEGE

Today when you hear about a college three-letter man, you wonder if it's LSD or POT!

College never hurt a man—unless, of course, he happened to be the student's father.

"Has your son's college education been of any tangible value?" inquired a friend.

"Oh yes. For one thing, it completely cured his mother of bragging about him."

The young man had just graduated from college and went to work in the family store. The first day his father asked him to sweep the sidewalk.

"But, Dad," he protested, "I'm a college graduate."

"I forgot about that," replied his father, "but don't worry. I'll show you how."

COLLEGE-BRED

A four-year loaf made with father's dough.

COLONEL SANDERS

A farmer vows he increased egg production by putting this sign in the henhouse: "An egg a day keeps Colonel Sanders away."

COMEBACK

Farmer: What are you doing in that tree, young man?

Boy: One of your apples fell down and I'm putting it back.

COMMERCIALS

Television commercials are the pause that depresses.

COMMON SENSE

Common sense is very uncommon. HORACE GREELEY

Common sense is the knack of seeing things as they are and doing things as they ought to be done. JOSH BILLINGS

COMMONWEALTH

A joint checking account.

COMMUNICATION

I know you believe you understand what you think I said, but I'm not sure you realize that what you heard is not what I meant.

COMPANIONS

Bad company is like a nail driven into a post, which, after the first or second blow, may be drawn out with little difficulty; but being once driven up to the head, the pincers cannot take hold to draw it out, but which can only be done by the destruction of the wood. AUGUSTINE

Keep good company, and you will be of the number. But if you keep company with bad men, their number will soon be increased by one.

CONCEIT

Conceit is God's gift to little men.

CONFIDENCE

Confidence of success is almost success.

CONGRATULATIONS

"Dear Emily, words cannot express how much I regret having broken off our engagement. Will you please come back to me? Your absence leaves a space no one can fill. Please forgive me and let us start all over again. I need you so much. Yours forever, Bob.

P.S. By the way, congratulations on winning the state lottery."

CONGRESSMEN

Put all our Congressmen together and they weigh about 96,000 pounds. It's hard to get anything that weighs 48 tons to move quickly.

CONQUER

Conquer a dog before you contend with a lion.

CONSCIENCE

Small boy's definition of conscience: "Something that makes you tell your mother before your sister does."

A clear conscience is a soft pillow.

CONTENTED

Our idea of a contented man is the one who enjoys the scenery along the detour.

CONVERSATION

A man's conversation is the mirror of his thoughts.

When there is a gap in the conversation, don't put your foot in it.

CONVERTED
You have not converted a man because you have silenced him.

CONVICTION
The difference between conviction and prejudice is that you can explain a conviction without getting angry.

COOKIES
Wife: I baked two kinds of cookies today. Would you like to take your pick?
Husband: No, thanks. I'll use my hammer.

COOKS
God sends us good meat, but the devil sends us cooks.

CORNS
As we grow older we don't feel our oats half as much as our corns.

CORRESPONDENCE
"Mary, where did you learn to sing?"
"I graduated from correspondence school."
"You must have missed a lot of mail."

COSMETICS
According to historians, women used cosmetics in the Middle Ages. And today women are still using cosmetics in the middle ages.

COST OF LIVING
Nowadays two can live as cheaply as one if both are working.

COUNSELORS
Plans go wrong with too few counselors; many counselors bring success. PROVERBS 15:22

COURAGE

Give us the fortitude to endure the things which cannot be changed, and the courage to change the things which should be changed, and the wisdom to know one from the other.

Last, but by no means least, courage—moral courage, the courage of one's convictions, the courage to see things through. The world is in a constant conspiracy against the brave. It's the age-old struggle—the roar of the crowd on one side and the voice of your conscience on the other. DOUGLAS MACARTHUR

One man with courage makes a majority. ANDREW JACKSON

COWARDICE

Cowards die many times before their deaths; the valiant never taste of death but once. WILLIAM SHAKESPEARE

CRABBY

It is better to live in the corner of an attic than with a crabby woman in a lovely home. PROVERBS 21:9

CRAZY

What a joke book writer is.

Joan: George is just crazy about me.
Jill: Don't take too much credit to yourself. He was crazy before you ever met him.

CRITICISM

The trouble with most of us is that we would rather be ruined by praise than saved by criticism.

Pay no attention to what critics say. There has never been a statue set up in honor of a critic.

Don't refuse to accept criticism; get all the help you can. PROVERBS 23:12

It is a badge of honor to accept valid criticism.
PROVERBS 25:12

If you refuse criticism you will end in poverty and disgrace; if you accept criticism you are on the road to fame. PROVERBS 13:18

No one so thoroughly appreciates the value of constructive criticism as the one who's giving it.

The public is the only critic whose opinion is worth anything at all. MARK TWAIN

Remember that nobody will ever get ahead of you as long as he is kicking you in the seat of the pants.
WALTER WINCHELL

CUPID

There is evidence that Cupid is a trapper as well as a hunter.

Brad: I hear Cupid almost got you last week.
Charlie: Yes, I had an arrow escape.

Cupid's darts hurt more coming out than going in.

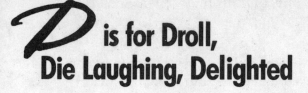 is for Droll,
Die Laughing, Delighted

DANCE

Rod: I'm through with that girl.
Doug: Why?
Rod: She asked me if I danced.
Doug: Well, what's wrong with that?
Rod: I was dancing with her when she asked me.

DATE

"I just had a date with a pair of Siamese twins."
"Did you have a good time?"
"Yes and no."

DEAD

"Do you believe it is possible to communicate with the dead?"
"Yes, I can hear you distinctly."

DEAF

Stewardess: I'm sorry, Mr. Jones, but we left your wife behind in Chicago.
Man: Thank goodness! For a moment there I thought I was going deaf!

DEAF-MUTE

Did you hear about the deaf-mute boy who used so many dirty words that his mother washed his hands with soap and water?

DEAFNESS

A scientist claims that loud rock music is beneficial in some cases of deafness. But then, deafness is beneficial in some cases of rock music.

DEEDS

Small deeds done are better than great deeds planned. PETER MARSHALL

DENTIST

One who lives from hand to mouth.

DESPERATION

The robber stuck a gun in the man's back, but the man turned suddenly, applied a judo grip, and flung him across the alley. Then he pounced on the robber and began to wipe him out. He blackened his eyes, broke his jaw, fractured his ribs, and broke both his arms. Finally the crook cried in desperation, "Hey, mister, ain't you never gonna call a cop?"

DIG

He who wants to dig will find a spade somewhere.

DINNER SPEAKER

A dinner speaker was in such a hurry to get to his engagement that when he arrived and sat down at the head table, he suddenly realized that he had forgotten his false teeth.

Turning to the man next to him he said, "I forgot my teeth." The man said, "No problem." With that he reached into his pocket and pulled out a pair of false teeth. "Try these," he said. The speaker tried them. "Too loose," he said. The man then said, "I have another pair—try these." The speaker tried them and responded, "Too tight." The man was not taken aback at all. He then said, "I have one more pair of false teeth—try them." The speaker said, "They fit perfectly." With that he ate his meal and gave his address.

After the dinner meeting was over, the speaker went over to thank the man who had helped him. "I want to thank you for coming to my aid. Where is your office? I've been looking for a good dentist."

The man replied, "I'm not a dentist. I'm an undertaker."

DISCUSS

Small minds discuss persons.
Average minds discuss events.
Great minds discuss ideas.

DISOBEY

A mother was having trouble with her children on one of those indoor days when it was raining outside. Finally the harassed mother turned on them and said, "All right, do anything you please. NOW LET ME SEE YOU DISOBEY THAT!"

DISTRUST

On one issue at least, men and women agree; they both distrust women.

DOCTOR

My doctor has an interesting approach to medicine. I open my wallet and he says, "Ah!"

The best doctors in the world are Doctor Diet, Doctor Quiet, and Doctor Merryman. JONATHAN SWIFT

Patient: Doctor, do you think cranberries are healthy?
Doctor: I've never heard one complain.

DO-IT-YOURSELF

A "do-it-yourself" catalog firm received the following letter from one of its customers:
I built a birdhouse according to your stupid plans, and not only is it much too big, it keeps blowing out of the tree. Signed, *Unhappy.*

The firm replied: *Dear Unhappy: We're sorry about the mix-up. We accidentally sent you a sailboat blueprint. But if you think you are unhappy, you should read the letter from the guy who came in last in the yacht club regatta in a leaky birdhouse.*

My husband is a do-it-yourself man. Every time I ask him to do something, he says, "Do it yourself."

DRIVING

"How long did it take your wife to learn to drive?"
"About two-and-a-half cars."

I came home last night, and there was a car in the dining room.
I said to my wife, "How did you get the car in the dining room?"
She said, "It was easy. I made a left turn when I came out of the kitchen."

Bill: Is your wife having any success in learning how to drive the car?
Jay: Well, the road is beginning to turn when she does.

DRUM

Something to buy for your enemy's children.

The first thing a child learns when he gets a drum is that he's never going to get another one.

DULL

One girl to another: "There's never a dull moment when you're out with Wilbur—it lasts the whole evening."

DUMB

"The Lord made us beautiful and dumb."

"How's that?"

"Beautiful so men would love us, and dumb so we could love them."

E is for Effervescence, Elation

EARACHE

A lady complained of an earache, so the doctor examined her and found a piece of string dangling from her right ear. The doctor began pulling it out, and the more he pulled, the more string came out. Suddenly the pulling became harder and he struggled with the string. To his amazement out fell a bouquet of roses.

The doctor exclaimed, "Good gracious, where did this come from?"

"How should I know?" said the patient. "Why don't you look at the card?"

ECSTASY

When all the children have grown up, married, and moved away, most parents experience a strange new emotion. It's called ecstasy.

EGOTIST

From all bad comes a little good. An egotist never goes around talking about other people.

ELBOWS

Rubbing elbows with a man will reveal things about him you never suspected. The same is true of rubbing fenders.

ELOQUENCE

Noise proves nothing. Often a hen who has merely laid an egg cackles as if she had laid an asteroid.

MARK TWAIN

The finest eloquence is that which gets things done.

EMBARRASSED

The young lady eyed her escort with great disapproval. "That's the fourth time you've gone back for more ice cream and cake, Albert," she said acidly. "Doesn't it embarrass you at all?"

"Why should it?" the hungry fellow said with a shrug. "I keep telling them I'm getting it for you."

Conceited: I can tell just by looking into a girl's eyes exactly how she feels about me.

Girl: Gee, that must be embarrassing for you.

EMPLOYMENT

When you hire people that are smarter than you are, you prove you are smarter than they are.

ENDANGERED

One national park ranger to another: "What do we do if we see an endangered animal eating an endangered plant?"

ENEMY

The Bible tells us to love our neighbors and also to love our enemies, probably because they are generally the same people.

ENGAGEMENT RING

Mary: Well, what happened when you showed the girls in the office your new engagement

ring? Did they all admire it?
Sara: Better than that—four of them recognized it!

ERR

To err is human, but to admit it is not.

ESCAPE

The news media featured a convict's daring daylight escape from prison and his voluntary return and surrender later that evening. When reporters asked him why he'd come back, he said, "The minute I sneaked home to see my wife, the first thing she said was, 'Where have you been? You escaped eight hours ago!'"

ESTIMATE

My wife spent four hours in the beauty shop the other day—and that was only for an estimate.

ETIQUETTE

Learning to yawn with your mouth closed.

EVIL

It is a sin to believe evil of another, but it is seldom a mistake.

EXAMPLE

Few things are harder to put up with than the annoyance of a good example. MARK TWAIN

He who lives well is the best preacher. MIGUEL DE CERVANTES

Preachers can talk but never teach,
Unless they practice what they preach.

When small men cast big shadows, it means the sun is about to set.

EXECUTE

Execute every act of thy life as though it were thy last. MARCUS AURELIUS

EXERCISE

A feeling that will go away if you just lie down for a little while.

EXPENSES

I never worry about meeting my expenses. I meet them whichever way I turn.

EXPLAIN

The man who takes time to explain his mistakes has little time left for anything else.

 **is for Funny, Farcical, Facetious**

FACE-LIFT

"My uncle had his face lifted."
"How did they do it?"
"With a piece of rope around his neck."

FAILURE

Never give a man up until he has failed at something he likes.

Failures are divided into two classes—those who thought and never did, and those who did and never thought.

Show me a thoroughly satisfied man and I will show you a failure. THOMAS A. EDISON

Failure is only the opportunity to begin again, more intelligently. HENRY FORD

A man can fail many times, but he isn't a failure in life until he begins to blame somebody else.

Life is a grindstone, and whether it grinds a man down or polishes him up depends on the stuff he's made of. JOSH BILLINGS

My great concern is not whether you have failed,
but whether you are content with your failure.
ABRAHAM LINCOLN

FAINTED

A man rose from his seat in a crowded bus so a lady
standing nearby could sit down. She was so
surprised she fainted.

When she revived and sat down, she said,
"Thanks."

Then the man fainted.

FAITH

Faith goes up the stairs that love has made and
looks out of the windows which hope has opened.
CHARLES HADDON SPURGEON

FALLING

Falling is easier than rising.

FAMILIARITY

Though familiarity may not breed contempt, it takes
the edge off of admiration.

FANATICISM

A fanatic is one who can't change his mind and
won't change the subject. WINSTON CHURCHILL

FAST

What you do while you try to get the waiter's
attention.

FATHER

It is a wonderful heritage to have an honest father.
PROVERBS 20:7

FEEBLE

"Darling, will you love me when I'm old and
feeble?"

"Yes, I do."

FILIBUSTER

The conversation of a bore.

FINE

A fine is a tax for doing wrong. A tax is a fine for doing well.

I'm fine, I'm fine.
There's nothing whatever the matter with me.
I'm just as healthy as I can be.
I have arthritis in both of my knees,
And when I talk, I talk with a wheeze.
My pulse is weak and my blood is thin,
But I'm awfully well for the shape I'm in.
My teeth eventually will have to come out,
And I can't hear a word unless you shout.
I'm overweight and I can't get thin,
But I'm awfully well for the shape I'm in.
Arch supports I have for both my feet
Or I wouldn't be able to walk down the street.
Sleep is denied me every night,
And every morning I'm really a sight.
My memory is bad and my head's a-spin,
And I practically live on aspirin,
But I'm awfully well for the shape I'm in.
The moral is, as this tale unfolds,
That for you and me who are growing old,
It's better to say, "I'm fine," with a grin
Than to let people know the shape we're in!

FINISH

He who begins many things finishes few.

FIRE

Sign on office bulletin board: In case of fire, don't panic. Simply flee the building with the same reckless abandon that occurs each day at quitting time.

FIREPROOF
Being related to the boss.

FISHING
Three-fourths of the earth's surface is water and one fourth is land. It's obvious that the good Lord intended that man should spend three times as much time fishing as plowing.

FLATTERY
Many who would fight if offered a bribe may be flattered into jumping off a house.

Fair words make me look to my purse.

Flattery is like cologne water: to be smelt of, not allowed. ABRAHAM LINCOLN

Flattery is a trap; evil men are caught in it, but good men stay away and sing for joy. PROVERBS 29:5-6

Flattery is a form of hatred and wounds cruelly. PROVERBS 26:28

FLEE
The wicked flee when no one is chasing them! But the godly are bold as lions! PROVERBS 28:1

FLEXIBILITY
The key to flexibility is indecision.

FLIRTING
"Did you ever catch your husband flirting?"
"Yes, that's the very way I did catch him."

FLOODED
Wife: Honey, I can't get the car started, I think it's flooded.
Husband: Where is it?
Wife: In the swimming pool.

FLOORWALKERS
Parents of a newborn baby.

FOOD
Square meals make round people.

FOOTBALL
The pastor of the Calvary Baptist Church in Tulsa
calls this his "football theology":

Draft choice:	Selection of a pew near to (or away from) air-conditioning vents.
Bench-warmer:	Inactive member.
In the pocket:	Where too many Christians keep their tithes.
Fumble:	Lousy sermon.
Two-minute warning:	Deacon in front row taking a peek at his watch in full view of the preacher.

FORGIVENESS
There is no revenge so complete as forgiveness.
JOSH BILLINGS

It is easier to forgive an enemy than a friend.

The weak can never forgive. Forgiveness is the
attribute of the strong. MAHATMA GANDHI

Forgiveness is the fragrance the violet sheds on the
heel that has crushed it. MARK TWAIN

FORTUNE
Wife to husband who just got off the scale: "Your
fortune says that you are handsome, chivalrous, and
wealthy. It even has your weight wrong!"

FRANKNESS
It is an honor to receive a frank reply. PROVERBS 24:26

In the end, people appreciate frankness more than
flattery. PROVERBS 28:23

FREEDOM
Freedom is not free. Free men are not equal. Equal
men are not free.

FRIEND

A friend is:
A PUSH when you've STOPPED,
A WORD when you're LONELY,
A GUIDE when you're SEARCHING,
A SMILE when you're SAD,
A SONG when you're GLAD.

Go often to the house of thy friend, for weeds choke up the unused path. WILLIAM SHAKESPEARE

FRUSTRATION

Trying to find your glasses without your glasses.

FUNERAL

"Do you believe in life after death?" the boss asked one of his younger employees.

"Yes, sir."

"Well, then, that makes everything just fine," the boss went on. "About an hour after you left yesterday to go to your grandfather's funeral, he stopped in to see you."

G is for Grin, Gag, Guffaw, Giggle, Goofy

GAMBLING

He who gambles picks his own pocket.

A minister was matching coins with a member of his congregation for a cup of coffee. When asked if that didn't constitute gambling, the minister replied, "It is merely a scientific method of determining just who is going to commit an act of charity."

GENEROSITY

If there be any truer measure of a man than by what he does, it must be what he gives.

GENIUS

Genius is one percent inspiration and ninety-nine percent perspiration. THOMAS A. EDISON

GERMS

Husband: Don't put that money in your mouth. There's germs on it.

Wife: Don't be silly. Even a germ can't live on the money you earn.

GIRLS

In the spring a young man's fancy lightly turns to what the girls have been seriously thinking of all winter.

GIVING

What you save, you leave behind; what you spend, you have for awhile, but what you give away, you take with you.

When you help the poor you are lending to the Lord—and he pays wonderful interest on your loan! PROVERBS 19:17

It is possible to give away and become richer! It is also possible to hold on too tightly and lose everything. Yes, the liberal man shall be rich! By watering others, he waters himself. PROVERBS 11:24-25

"Give until it hurts."
   "Here's a quarter."
   "You can't stand much pain, can you?"

GOD

Sunday school teacher: Why do you believe in God?
Small student: I guess it just runs in our family.

GOLF

Peggy: You think so much of your old golf game, you probably don't even remember when we were married.
Lowell: Of course I do, my dear. It was the day I sank that thirty-foot putt.

GOOD OLD DAYS

Too many people keep looking forward to the good old days.

1880 . . . "I walked fourteen miles through snow and rain to go to school."
1915 . . . "I had to walk five miles every day."

1936 . . . "It was eleven blocks to the bus stop every
          morning."
1950 . . . "I had to buy gasoline for my own car."
1966 . . . "When I drove to school as a boy, we didn't
          have power brakes, power steering, or
          power windows."

GOSSIP

Meddle not with dirt; some of it will stick to your
fingers.

Not everyone repeats gossip. Some improve it.

If nobody listened, to whom would gossips talk?

Gossips are the spies of life.

The only time people dislike gossip is when you
gossip about them. WILL ROGERS

None are so fond of secrets as those who do not
mean to keep them.

GRACE

One blistering hot day when the family had guests
for dinner, the mother asked four-year-old Johnny
to say grace. "But I don't know what to say," the boy
said.

   "Oh, just say what you hear me say," the mother
replied.

   Obediently, the boy bowed his head and
murmured, "Oh, Lord, why did I invite these people
here on a hot day like this?"

GRAFFITI

Wit-and-run literature.

GROAN

The result of reading this joke book.

GROUCH

She avoids getting up with a grouch. She rises
before he does.

GROUP THERAPY

Did you hear about those new group-therapy luncheons? They are called "Whining and Dining."

GROWLS

Ken: Does your father have a den?
Melba: He doesn't need one. He just growls all over the house.

GUILT

Every guilty person is his own hangman. SENECA

GURU

Guru to guest: "There are several meanings of life—a fifty-dollar meaning, a one-hundred-dollar meaning, and a very meaningful five-hundred-dollar meaning."

H is for Hilarity, Humor, Health, Heehaw

HABIT

Habit, if not resisted, soon becomes necessity.
AUGUSTINE

The unfortunate thing about this world is that the good habits are much easier to give up than the bad ones. W. SOMERSET MAUGHAM

Sow an act and you reap a habit.
Sow a habit and you reap a character.
Sow a character and you reap a destiny.
CHARLES READE

Habit is habit and not to be flung out of the window by any man, but coaxed downstairs a step at a time.
MARK TWAIN

Habits are cobwebs first, cables at last.

HAIR COLOR

They say brunettes have a sweeter disposition than blonds and redheads. Don't believe it. My wife has been all three, and I couldn't see any difference.

HANGED

The applicant for life insurance was finding it difficult to fill out the application. The salesman asked what the trouble was, and the man said that he couldn't answer the question about the cause of death of his father.

The salesman wanted to know why. After some embarrassment the client explained that his father had been hanged.

The salesman pondered for a moment. "Just write: 'Father was taking part in a public function when the platform gave way.'"

HAPPY

Ken: For eighteen long years my girl and I were deliriously happy.
Bob: Then what happened?
Ken: We met.

HAT

His name was "Seven-and-a-quarter." They had picked his name out of a hat.

HEROISM

The main thing about being a hero is to know when to die. WILL ROGERS

HIGH HEELS

The invention of a woman who had been kissed on the forehead.

HIPPOPOTAMUS

The teacher took her class to the zoo. When they passed the lion's cage, she asked, "What's the plural of lion?"

One of the boys answered, "Lions."

"What's the plural of sheep?" she asked.

One of the girls answered, "Sheep."

A little farther along they came upon a hippopotamus.

"What's the plural of hippopotamus?" the teacher asked little Johnny.

Johnny shuddered. "Who would want two of those?"

HOBBY

Voluntary work.

HOME

Home is where you can be silent and still be heard ... where you can ask and find out who you are ... where people laugh with you about yourself ... where sorrow is divided and joy multiplied ... where we share and love and grow.

Nothing makes you feel that your home is your castle more than getting an estimate to have it painted.

HONEYMOON

The vacation a man takes before beginning work under a new boss.

HORN

The horn of plenty is the one the guy behind you has on his car.

HORSERADISH

A minister who was very fond of pure, hot horseradish always kept a bottle of it on his dining room table. He offered some to a guest, who took a big bite.

When the guest finally was able to speak, he gasped, "I've heard many preach hellfire, but you are the first one I've met who passed out a sample of it."

HORSE SENSE

It takes horse sense and stable thinking to stay hitched these days.

HORSE STEALING

Teacher: Name one of the benefits of the
automotive age.
Student: It has practically stopped horse stealing.

HUMOR

If I had no sense of humor, I would long ago have
committed suicide. MAHATMA GANDHI

There are very few good judges of humor, and they
don't agree. JOSH BILLINGS

HYPOCHONDRIAC

One who enjoys poor health.

HYPOCRITE

The man who murdered both his parents and then
pleaded for mercy on the grounds that he was an
orphan. ABRAHAM LINCOLN

I is for Inventive, Idiocy, Intense Laughter

IDEAL HUSBAND

WHAT EVERY WOMAN EXPECTS
He will be a brilliant conversationalist.
He will be very sensitive, kind, understanding, truly
   loving.
He will be a very hard-working man.
He will help around the house by washing dishes,
   vacuuming floors, and taking care of the yard.
He will help his wife raise the children.
He will be a man of emotional and physical
   strength.
He will be as smart as Einstein, but will look like
   Robert Redford.

WHAT SHE GETS
He always takes her to the best restaurants.
(Someday he may even take her inside.)
He doesn't have any ulcers—he gives them.
Anytime he gets an idea in his head, he has the
   whole thing in a nutshell.
He's well-known as a miracle worker—it's a
   miracle when he works.

He supports his wife in the manner to which she was accustomed—he's letting her keep her job.

He's such a bore that he even bores you to death when he gives you a compliment.

He has occasional flashes of silence that make his conversation brilliant.

IDEAL WIFE

WHAT EVERY MAN EXPECTS

She will always be beautiful and cheerful. She could marry a movie star, but wants only you.

She will have hair that never needs curlers or beauty shops.

Her beauty won't run in a rainstorm.

She will never be sick—just allergic to jewelry and fur coats.

She will insist that moving the furniture by herself is good for her figure.

She will be an expert in cooking, cleaning house, fixing the car or TV, painting the house, and keeping quiet.

Her favorite hobbies will be mowing the lawn and shoveling snow.

She will hate charge cards.

Her favorite expression will be, "What can I do for you, dear?"

She will think you have Einstein's brain but look like Mr. America.

She will wish you would go out with the boys so she could get some sewing done.

She will love you because you're so sexy.

WHAT HE GETS

She speaks 140 words a minute, with gusts up to 180.

She was once a model for a totem pole.

She is a light eater—as soon as it gets light, she starts eating.

Where there's smoke, there she is—cooking.
She lets you know you only have two faults—
   everything you say and everything you do.
No matter what she does with it, her hair looks like
   an explosion in a steel wool factory.
If you get lost, open your wallet—she'll find you.

IDENTITY CRISIS

A lot of people don't realize they have an identity
crisis until they try to cash a check in a strange
town.

IDIOT

Q: What do they call a fellow who introduces his
   best girl to his best friend?
A: An idiot.

IMITATION

"I'm rather good at imitations. I can imitate almost
any bird you can name."
   "How about a homing pigeon?"

INDEPENDENT

Rod: Are you independent on your new job?
Ron: I should say so! I go to work anytime I want to
   before seven and quit anytime I get ready after
   five o'clock.

INSANITY

Insanity is hereditary: you can get it from your
children. SAM LEVENSON

Insanity destroys reason, but not wit.

INSURANCE

Jack: Don't you know you can't sell insurance
   without a license?
Buck: I knew I wasn't selling any, but I didn't know
   the reason.

The following quotations were taken from a
Toronto newspaper. They are samples of comments

that individuals wrote down on their claim forms
following their auto accidents.

I misjudged a lady crossing the street.
Coming home, I drove into the wrong house and
  collided with a tree I don't have.
I collided with a stationary streetcar coming in the
  opposite direction.
The other car collided with mine without giving
  warning of its intentions.
I heard a horn blow and was struck in the back—a
  lady was evidently trying to pass me.
I thought my window was down, but found it was up
  when I put my hand through it.
My car was stolen, and I sent up a hue and cry but it
  has not been recovered.
I collided with a stationary truck coming the other
  way.
The truck backed through my windshield into my
  wife's face.
A pedestrian hit me and went under my car.
The guy was all over the road. I had to swerve a
  number of times before I hit him.
If the other driver had stopped a few yards behind
  himself, the accident would not have happened.
In my attempt to kill a fly, I drove into a telephone
  pole.
I had been shopping for plants all day, and was on
  my way home. As I reached an intersection, a
  hedge sprang up, obscuring my vision.
I did not see the other car.
I had been driving my car for forty years when I fell
  asleep at the wheel and had an accident.
I was on my way to the doctor's with rear end
  trouble when my universal joint gave way, causing
  me to have an accident.
My car was legally parked as it backed into the
  other vehicle.

An invisible car came out of nowhere, struck my
vehicle, and vanished.

I told the police that I was not injured, but on
removing my hat, I found that I had a skull
fracture.

I was sure the old fellow would never make it to the
other side of the road when I struck him.

The pedestrian had no idea which way to go, so I
ran over him.

The indirect cause of this accident was a little guy
in a small car with a big mouth.

I was thrown from my car as it left the road. I was
later found in a ditch by some stray cows.

The telephone pole was approaching fast. I was
attempting to swerve out of its path when it struck
my front end.

I was unable to stop in time, and my car crashed
into the other vehicle. The driver and passengers
then left immediately for a vacation with injuries.

I pulled away from the side of the road, glanced at
my mother-in-law, and headed over the
embankment.

INTRODUCTION

I am not going to stand here and tell you a lot of old
jokes . . . but I will introduce the speaker tonight
who will.

IRS

Behind every successful man is a representative of
the Internal Revenue Service.

IT'S A BOY

An unmarried girl who works in a busy office
arrived early one morning and began passing out
cigars and candy, both tied with blue ribbons. When
asked what the occasion was, she proudly displayed
a diamond solitaire on her third finger, left hand,
and announced: "It's a boy—six feet tall and 187
pounds."

J is for Jest, Jolly, Joke, Jocularity

JOKE

A form of humor enjoyed by some and misunderstood by most.

Thou canst not joke an enemy into a friend, but thou mayst jolt a friend into an enemy.

JUDGMENT

Husband: But you must admit that men have better judgment than women.

Wife: Oh yes—you married me, and I married you.

JUNK

The proliferation of garage sales leads us to suspect that the whole economy is sustained by everybody else's junk.

 is for Kooky

KAYAK

Two Eskimos sitting in a kayak were chilly, but when they lit a fire in the craft it sank— proving once and for all that you can't have your kayak and heat it, too.

KISSING

A kiss is a peculiar proposition—of no use to one, yet absolute bliss to two. The small boy gets it for nothing, the young man has to lie for it, and the old man has to buy it. It is the baby's right, the lover's privilege, and the hypocrite's mask. To a young girl, it shows faith; to a married woman, hope; and to an old maid, charity.

Girl: Did you kiss me when the lights were out?
Boy: No!
Girl: It must have been that fellow over there!
Boy (starting to get up): I'll teach him a thing or
      two!
Girl: You couldn't teach him a thing!

"May I kiss you?"
  Silence.

"May I please kiss you?"
Silence.
"Are you deaf?"
"No, are you paralyzed?"

Father: When I was your age, I never kissed a girl.
Will you be able to tell your children that?
Son: Not with a straight face.

You can't kiss a girl unexpectedly—only sooner
than she thought you would.

Kissing shortens life—single life.

KITCHEN

Bob: Somehow I don't think my wife knows her
way around the kitchen.
Ray: Why do you say that?
Bob: This morning I saw her trying to open an egg
with a can opener.

L is for Levity, Laughter, Lighthearted, Ludicrous, Loony

LAST MINUTE
If it weren't for the last minute, a lot of things wouldn't get done.

LATE
Mother: Why so late coming home from school?
Boy: The bus driver broke down.

LAW
The best way to get a bad law repealed is to enforce it strictly. ABRAHAM LINCOLN

LAZINESS
The mother of invention.

LEAD
He's rich. He's got gold in California, silver in New Mexico, but the lead is still in the same place.

LEARNING
Men learn while they teach. SENECA

LEISURE
Leisure is a beautiful garment, but it will not do for constant wear.

LETTER

Ken: Did you hear that God is very angry with the sinfulness of man and is going to destroy all of the wicked? But before he does, he has sent a very special letter to all the good and righteous people. Do you know what the letter says?

Bob: No, what?

Ken: You mean you didn't get one?

LICENSE

The typical American boy learns to walk within a year, and forgets how to do so immediately upon securing a driver's license.

The traffic officer ordered the motorist to pull up to the curb and show his driver's license.

"I don't understand this, officer, I haven't done anything wrong."

"No, you haven't, but you were driving so carefully I thought you might not have your license."

LINGUIST

"I hear your husband is a linguist."

"Yes, he speaks three languages—golf, football, and baseball."

LITTLE THINGS

Little leaks sink great ships.

LOCKJAW

The best thing for bad breath.

LOST

Hungry and exhausted, a hunter stumbled forward, throwing his arms around the man who emerged from a thicket. He cried, "Am I glad to see you! I've been lost for two days."

"What are you so glad about? I've been lost a week!"

LOVE

Guy: Margie, I love you! I love you, Margie!
Gal: In the first place, you don't love me, and in the second place, my name isn't Margie.

Girl: Do you love me?
Boy: Yes, dear.
Girl: Would you die for me?
Boy: No—mine is an undying love.

Love is sometimes like a poisoned mushroom. You can't tell if it's the real thing until it's too late.

 **is for Merry, Mirthful, Mindless**

MAN OF THE YEAR
Melba: My husband was named Man of the Year.
Pam: Well, that shows you what kind of a year it's been.

MARRIAGE
A man who thinks he is more intelligent than his wife is married to a smart woman.

Marriage counselor to his wife: Maybe your problem is that you've been waking up grumpy in the morning.
Wife: No, I always let him sleep.

Wife: When we were younger, you used to nibble on my ear.
Husband: Excuse me. I'll be right back.
Wife: Where are you going?
Husband: I'm going to get my teeth.

Wife: At least you could read to me while I sew.
Husband: Why don't you sew to me while I read?

Wife: Before we were married, we didn't sit this far apart in the car.
Husband: Well, dear, I didn't move.

"We've been married for fifty years."
"How does it feel?"
"Who feels after fifty years?"

Son: How much does it cost to get married, Dad?
Dad: I don't know. I'm still paying on it.

Some people ask the secret of our long marriage.
We take time to go to a restaurant two times a week.
A little candlelight, dinner, soft music, and a slow
walk home. She goes Tuesdays; I go Fridays.

Sue: See that woman over there? She's been
married four times—once to a millionaire, then
to an actor, then to a minister, and last to an
undertaker.
Sal: I know! One for the money, two for the show,
three to get ready, and four to go!

Marriage is like a violin—after the music stops, the
strings are still attached.

A deaf husband and a blind wife are always a happy
couple.

The cooing usually stops when the honeymoon is
over, but billing goes on forever.

A marriage certificate is a legal paper that lets guys
keep the game in captivity after the hunting season
is over.

Marriage is nature's way of keeping people from
fighting with strangers.

Marriage is like a railroad sign—first you stop, then
you look, then you listen.

Marriage is like a midnight phone call—you get a
ring and then you wake up.

Love is blind, and marriage is an eye-opener.

Marriage is like a bathtub—once you are in it for
awhile, it's not so hot.

Boy: Will you marry me?
Girl: No, but I'll always admire your good taste.

He: What would you say if I asked you to marry me?
She: Nothing. I can't talk and laugh at the same time.

Boy: I would like to marry you.
Girl: Well, leave your name and address, and if nothing better turns up, I will notify you.

He: What can I say that will convince you of my love and cause you to marry me?
She: Only three little words.

MEMORIES

God gave us our memories so that we might have roses in December.

Pleasant memories must be arranged for in advance.

MENTAL ILLNESS

Is mental illness contagious? There seems to be a lot of it going around.

MIDDLE AGE

Middle age is when your memory is shorter, experience longer, stamina lower, and your forehead higher.

In middle age you are as young as ever, but it takes a lot more effort.

MINISTER

After his return from church one Sunday, a small boy said, "You know what, Mommy? I'm going to be a minister when I grow up."

"That's fine," said his mother. "But what made you decide you want to be a preacher?"

"Well," said the boy pensively, "I'll have to go to church on Sunday anyway, and I think it would be more fun to stand up and yell than to sit still and listen."

MISER

A miser is a rich pauper.

MISJUDGED

Wife: I should have taken my mother's advice and never married you! How she tried to stop me!

Husband: Holy mackerel, how I've misjudged that woman!

MONEY

Wife: I think you only married me because my daddy left me a lot of money.

Husband: That's not true. I didn't care who left you the money.

Husband: What have you been doing with all the grocery money I gave you?

Wife: Turn sideways and look in the mirror.

MOSES

Teacher: You can be sure that if Moses were alive today, he'd be considered a remarkable man.

Lenny: He sure ought to be—he'd be more than 2,500 years old.

MOTHER

Every boy who has a dog should also have a mother, so the dog will be fed regularly.

Husband: Now look, Lucy. I don't want to seem harsh, but your mother has been living with us for twenty years now. Don't you think it's time she got a place of her own?

Wife: *My* mother? I thought she was *your* mother.

MOTHER-IN-LAW

The mother-in-law frequently forgets that she was once a daughter-in-law.

A man was told by his neighbor that his domineering mother-in-law had just died. The man remained expressionless, apparently unaffected by the news.

"Your mother-in-law has just died, and you show no expression at all?"

"If you had a toothache like I do, you'd have trouble smiling, too."

A married couple was having their weekly fight concerning their families.

"You never say anything nice about my family," the wife complained.

"Yes, I do," her husband replied. "I said I think your mother-in-law is a lot nicer than mine."

Did you hear about the man who was driving down the street, when all of a sudden he came across a long line of people. They were all walking single file in the middle of the road. He drove past a hundred, then two hundred, then three hundred, until he lost count. All of them were walking single file down the yellow line in the center of the street.

Finally, up ahead he saw the line of people slowing down to a standstill. At the head of the line he saw a hearse, and then another hearse, and then a big black limousine. The limousine had a flat tire and the driver was changing the tire. The man's curiosity was so great that he pulled his car over to the side of the road, got out, walked over to the limousine, and knocked on the window.

The window rolled down, and he saw a man in a black suit, and next to him on the seat was a dog. Finally, the man spoke to the fellow in the black suit. "Pardon me, sir," he said, "but I have never seen a funeral like this before. Could you tell me what is going on?"

The man in the suit replied, "Well, in the first hearse is my wife. The dog sitting next to me killed her."

"Oh, I'm terribly sorry," said the man. "But what about the second hearse?"

The man in the suit said, "In the second hearse is my mother-in-law, and the dog next to me killed her also."

"I'm so sorry," said the man. He then started to walk back to his car. About halfway there, he turned around and went back to the limousine. He said, "Excuse me, sir, but would it be possible to borrow your dog for awhile?"

The man in the black suit replied, "Get in line."

MOUTH

A closed mouth catches no flies.

Mary's mouth costs her nothing, for she never opens it but at others' expense.

MOZART

A married couple trying to live up to a snobbish life-style went to a party. The conversation turned to Mozart. "Absolutely brilliant, magnificent, a genius!"

The woman, wanting to join in the conversation, remarked casually, "Ah, Mozart. You're so right. I love him. Only this morning I saw him getting on the No. 5 bus going to Coney Island." There was a sudden hush, and everyone looked at her. Her husband was mortified. He pulled her away and whispered, "We're leaving right now. Get your coat and let's get out of here."

As they drove home, he kept muttering to himself. Finally his wife turned to him. "You're angry about something."

"Oh, really? You noticed?" he sneered. "I've never been so embarrassed in my life! You saw Mozart take the No. 5 bus to Coney Island? You idiot! Don't you know the No. 5 bus doesn't go to Coney Island?"

MUD

Mud thrown is ground lost.

MUD PACKS

"Every once in a while my wife puts on one of those mud packs."

"Does it improve her looks?"

"Only for a few days—then the mud falls off."

MUSHROOMS

"Did you hear about the guy who had three wives in three months? The first two died of poisoned mushrooms."

"What happened to the third wife?"

"She died from a blow on the head. She wouldn't eat the mushrooms!"

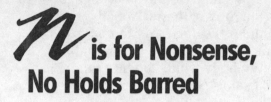 is for Nonsense, No Holds Barred

NAG

A motorist was complaining about his car. "It has a buzzer that tells me my seat belt isn't fastened, another that warns when my speed is over sixty-five, and a light that tells me when my gas is low. My wife isn't bad enough—now my dashboard nags me!"

NARROW-ESCAPE

She was going to have an announcement party, but the engagement was broken, so she went ahead and called it a narrow-escape party.

NEGLECT

A little neglect may breed great mischief. BENJAMIN FRANKLIN

NERVOUS

All that stops most of us from having a nervous breakdown these days is that we can't afford it.

NEWLYWED

Newlywed couples shouldn't expect the first few meals to be perfect. After all, it takes time to find the right restaurant.

NEXT

A fellow went to a psychiatrist and said, "Doctor, I don't know what's wrong with me. Nobody wants to talk to me. My employees don't talk to me, my children don't talk to me, my wife doesn't talk to me. Why is it that nobody wants to talk to me?"

The psychiatrist said, "Next!"

NODDING

Following a lot of dull, long-winded speakers at a sports dinner, a well-known athlete, noticing some guests who had dozed off, started his speech: "Friends and nodding acquaintances."

NOTHING

Most of us know *how* to say nothing; few of us know *when*.

Between the great things that we cannot do and the small things we will not do, the danger is that we shall do nothing.

He who is doing nothing is seldom without helpers.

"What are you doing, Joe?"
"Nothing, sir," was his reply.
"And you there, Tom, pray let me know?"
"I'm busy, sir—I'm helping Joe."
"Is nothing, then, so hard to do,
That thus it takes the time of two?"
"No," said the other with a smile,
And grinned and chuckled all the while;
"But we're such clever folks, d'ye see.
That nothing's hard to Joe and me."

 is for Outrageous, Oh, How Funny

OBESITY

Obesity in this country is really widespread.

OBEY

She: In most marriage ceremonies they don't use the word *obey* anymore.

He: Too bad, isn't it? It used to lend a little humor to the occasion.

OBOE

An English tramp.

OBSERVANT

Did you hear about the observant chap who claims to have discovered the color of the wind? He went out and found it blew.

OIL

A little oil may save a deal of friction.

OLD MAID

Slipping beauty.

Old maid's laughter: He! he! he!

OPERATION

Operations are so common these days that you can hardly work yours into the conversation unless it is fatal.

OPINION

People do not seem to realize that their opinion of the world is also a confession of character. RALPH WALDO EMERSON

OPTIMIST

Twixt optimist and pessimist
The difference is droll.
The optimist sees the donut,
The pessimist the hole.

Question: What do they call a man who runs the motor of his car while waiting for his wife?

Answer: An optimist.

ORDER

Two dangers constantly threaten the world: order and disorder.

ORIGINALITY

Many a man fails as an original thinker simply because his memory is too good.

OVEREATING

The only thing harder than giving up overeating is trying to keep from telling everyone how you did it.

OVERPOPULATION

Wife: This article on overpopulation of the world says that somewhere in the world there is a woman having a baby every four seconds!

Husband: I think they ought to find that woman and stop her!

 **is for Playful, Puns**

PAIL
God gives the milk but not the pail.

PAIN IN THE NECK
Becky: Hello, dear. How's the pain in the neck?
Pam: He's out golfing.

PALM READER
Sally: Well, I'm falling in love, and I think I should go to a palm reader or a mind reader. Which would you suggest?
Hallie: You'd better go to a palm reader—you know you've got a palm.

PANTYHOSE
One father to another: "My daughter is in that awkward age. She tore her pantyhose while hunting Easter eggs."

PARENTS
The first half of our lives is ruined by our parents and the second half by our children. CLARENCE DARROW

The most important thing a father can do for his children is to love their mother.

Advice to parents: Don't be hard on the children when they fight; they may be just playing house.

PAYMENT

He who dances must pay the fiddler—also the waiter, the porter, the hat check girl, the doorman, and the parking lot attendant.

PEANUT BUTTER

The school cafeteria had a breakdown in the kitchen and served peanut butter and jelly sandwiches instead of the usual hot meal. After lunch a satisfied second-grader complimented the cafeteria manager: "Finally you gave us a home-cooked meal!"

PELTS

He that pelts every barking dog must pick up a great many stones.

PERFECTION

One thing I'll say for my wife, she's a very neat housekeeper. If I drop my socks on the floor, she picks them up. If I throw my clothes around, she hangs them up. I got up at three o'clock the other morning and went into the kitchen to get a glass of orange juice, and when I came back, I found the bed made.

PERFORMER

He isn't the kind of a performer that "stops a show" ... but I have often seen him "slow it down."

PERPETUAL MOTION

The people in the apartment above.

PERSONAL LOAN

The reason banks refer to them as personal loans is

that when you miss a payment, the banks get personal.

PIANO

Wife: I simply can't understand why you always sit on the piano stool whenever we have company. Everyone knows that you can't play a note.

Husband: I know it, dear. And as long as I'm sitting there, neither can anybody else.

PIGS

Pigs grunt about everything and nothing.

"He said you weren't fit to sleep with the pigs."

"And I suppose you pulled the old gag and said I was?"

"No, I stuck up for the pigs."

PINCH

As the crowded elevator descended, Mrs. Wilson became increasingly furious with her husband, who was delighted to be pressed against a gorgeous blonde.

As the elevator stopped at the main floor, the blonde suddenly whirled, slapped Mr. Wilson, and said, "That will teach you to pinch!"

Bewildered, Mr. Wilson was halfway to the parking lot with his wife when he choked, "I-I didn't pinch that girl."

"Of course you didn't," said his wife. "I did."

PIRATE SHIP

A pirate ship is a thugboat.

PLACE

The modern husband believes a woman's place is in the home—and expects her to go there immediately after work.

PLANNING

It is pleasant to see plans develop. That is why fools refuse to give them up even when they are wrong.
PROVERBS 13:19

Any enterprise is built by wise planning, becomes strong through common sense, and profits wonderfully by keeping abreast of the facts.
PROVERBS 24:3-4

POD

They get along like two peeves in a pod.

POISON

"I'd like to die by poison."
"I'd like to be killed by kindness."
"It's easier to get poison."

POLITICIANS

Local café and restaurant owners expected a boost in business when the politicians arrived for the convention. "Let's hope," said one restauranteur, "that they spend their money the way they spend ours."

POLLUTION

Man at a lunch counter: "My new apartment has windows on all sides, so I get cross-pollution."

A woman who recently moved to Columbia, South Carolina, after living for forty-eight years in New York says she loves everything about the capital city and South Carolina, with one exception: "How," she asks, with tongue in check, "can you people dare breathe something you can't see? I find it a little scary myself."

POLYGAMY

This country will never adopt polygamy. The divorce courts couldn't stand the strain.

POPULARITY
Avoid popularity if you would have peace.
ABRAHAM LINCOLN

POSITIVE
"Are you positive?"
  "Only fools are positive."
  "Are you sure?"
  "I'm positive."

POT
I set out in life to find the pot of gold at the end of the rainbow. Now I'm sixty and all I've got is the pot.

POVERTY
A little girl who lived in a wealthy suburb was asked to write a story about a poor family. She began the story this way: "The family was very poor. The mommy was poor, the daddy was poor. Brothers and sisters were poor. The maid was poor, the nurse was poor, the butler was poor, the cook was poor, and the yardman was poor."

A man can stand his own poverty better than he can the other fellow's prosperity.

Why do people try so hard to conceal poverty at the time they are experiencing it, and then brag about it so much in their memoirs?

PRAYER
If prayers were puddings, many men would starve.

PREACHERS
Someone who talks in another person's sleep.

Preacher: A lot of people must be sick with colds. There was sure a great deal of coughing during my sermon this morning.
Deacon: Those were time signals.

PREDICT

Sammy: Do you think anyone can predict the future with cards?

Danny: My mother can. She takes one look at my report cards, then tells me exactly what will happen when my dad gets home.

PREJUDICE

Prejudice is a great time-saver. It enables us to form opinions without bothering with facts.

You can sway a thousand men by appealing to their prejudices quicker than you can convince one man by logic.

PRESCRIPTIONS

I finally figured out what doctors scribble on those prescriptions: "I've got my twenty bucks, now you get yours."

PRESIDENT

When I was a boy I was told that anybody could become president; I'm beginning to believe.
CLARENCE DARROW

PRETENSION

The hardest tumble a man can make is to fall over his own bluff.

PRETTY

He: The more I look at you, the prettier you get.

She: Oh?

He: I ought to look at you more often.

PRIDE

One of the best temporary cures for pride and affection is seasickness; a man who wants to vomit never puts on airs. JOSH BILLINGS

Did you hear about the man who had a gold tooth that was the pride of his life? He got in a fight the other day and someone hit him in the mouth. He had to swallow his pride.

PROCRASTINATION

By the street of By-and-By, one arrives at the house of Never. MIGUEL DE CERVANTES

PRODUCTION

A man of words and not of deeds
Is like a garden full of weeds.

PROMISES

Bob: I would go to the end of the world for you!
Pam: Yes, but would you stay there?

PSYCHIATRIST

Rodney Dangerfield says his cousin went to a psychiatrist because he felt he was ugly. "The psychatrist almost had my cousin convinced he wasn't ugly," the comedian said, "but he spoiled it all by making him lie on the couch face down."

PSYCHOPATH

Bob: Do you know what a psychopath is?
Bill: Sure, that's a path where psychos walk up and
down.

PUNCTUAL

The trouble with being punctual is that there's nobody there to appreciate it.

Nothing makes an office worker more punctual than 5:00 P.M.

PURPOSE

Working without method, like the pig's tail, goes all day and does nothing.

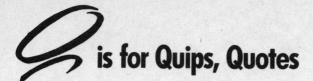 **is for Quips, Quotes**

QUIET

Quiet people aren't the only ones who don't say much.

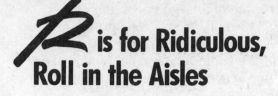is for Ridiculous, Roll in the Aisles

RAISE

Dean: Why do you ask for a raise?
Assistant professor: Well, sir, I wouldn't ask for a raise, but somehow my kids found out that other families eat three times a day.

"Got anything to say before I fire you?"
"Yeah. How about a raise?"

READING

Reading is to the mind what exercise is to the body.
JOSEPH ADDISON

The man who doesn't read good books has no advantage over the man who can't read them.

REDUCING

"My wife has been using a flesh-reducing roller for nearly two months."
"And can you see any result yet?"
"Yes—the roller is much thinner."

RELATIVES

Inherited critics.

REPETITION

The professor of English was trying to drum into his class the importance of a large vocabulary.

"I assure you," he said, "if you repeat a word ten or twelve times, it will be yours forever."

In the back of the room a cute coed took a deep breath, closed her eyes and whispered, "Richard, Richard, Richard. . . ."

REPRIMAND

Bill: Did you reprimand your little boy for mimicking me?

Sharon: Yes, I told him not to act like a fool.

REPUTATION

If you must choose, take a good name rather than great riches; for to be held in loving esteem is better than silver and gold. PROVERB 22:1

Glass, china, and reputation are easily cracked, and never well mended.

RESORT

I just heard of a man who met his wife at a travel bureau. She was looking for a vacation, and he was the last resort.

RESPONSIBILITY

The highest praise for a man is to give him responsibility.

RIDE

Two men ride a horse, but one must ride behind.

RIGHT

The trouble with doing something right the first time is that nobody appreciates how difficult it was.

ROBIN HOOD

Talk like Robin Hood when you can shoot his bow.

RUBBER BAND

In the bank one day a little boy suddenly called out at the top of his voice, "Did anyone drop a roll of bills with a rubber band around it?"

Several people at different tellers' windows answered, "I did!"

"Well, I just now found the rubber band," said the boy.

RULE THE WORLD

Husband: I know you're having a lot of trouble with the baby, dear, but keep in mind, "The hand that rocks the cradle is the hand that rules the world."

Wife: Well, in that case, would you mind taking over the world while I go shopping?

S is for Silly, Sidesplitting, Snicker

SALESMAN

Brad: I'm an independent salesman.
Dave: Really?
Brad: Yes. I take orders from no one.

SATISFACTION

A man sitting at his window one evening casually called to his wife: "There goes that woman Ken Roberts is in love with."

His wife in the kitchen dropped the plate she was drying, ran into the living room, knocked over a vase, and looked out the window.

"Where, where?" she asked.

"Over there," said the husband. "The woman in the blue dress standing on the corner."

"Why, you big idiot," she replied, "that's his wife."

"Yes, of course," answered the husband with a satisfied grin.

SATISFIED

Lawyer (handing check for $100 to client who had been awarded $5,000): There's the balance after deducting my fee. What's the matter? Aren't you satisfied?

Client: I was just wondering who got hit by the car—you or me.

SAWMILL

Ken: I slept like a log.
Melba: Yes, I heard the sawmill.

SEAFOOD DIET

My husband is on a seafood diet. Every time he sees food, he eats.

SELFISHNESS

He who lives only to benefit himself confers on the world a benefit when he dies. TERTULLIAN

SENTENCE

Judge: Twenty days or twenty dollars.
Prisoner: I'll take the money, your honor.

SEPARATION

Bob: Time separates the best of friends.
Bill: So does money.
Ken: And don't forget marriage.

SLEEP

A clothing manufacturer, so worried that he couldn't sleep, was advised by his business associates to count sheep. Next day the man appeared more exhausted than ever. "Sure, I counted sheep," he told his associates. "I counted up to 20,000. Then I began figuring: Those 20,000 sheep would produce 80,000 pounds of wool—enough to make 30,000 yards of cloth. That would make 12,000 overcoats. Man! Who could sleep with an inventory like that?"

SMART:

Q: A man who always remembers a woman's birthday but forgets her age is called what?
A: A smart man.

SMILE

If you see someone without a smile, give him one of
yours.

SMOKE

Jay: Does the Bible say that if you smoke you can't
get to heaven?

Bufe: No, but the more you smoke the quicker
you'll get there.

SNORE

How come people who snore always fall asleep
first?

SOWING AND REAPING

Sow a thought, you reap an act.
Sow an act, you reap a habit.
Sow a habit, you reap a character.
Sow a character, you reap a destiny.

SPACE

Boastful soldier at a party: The bullet struck my
head and went careening into space.

Bored friend: You're being honest about it,
anyway.

SPEAK

"Did you ever hear me speak?"
"I never heard you do anything else."

SPEAKING

A speechmaker's closing remark: "I have a lot more
to say, but I try to observe the first rule of public
speaking: Nice guys finish fast!"

SPEECH

The many quips from Sir Winston Churchhill are
legendary. One of our favorites is when he was
asked, "Doesn't it thrill you to know that every
time you make a speech the hall is packed to
overflowing?"

"It is quite flattering," Sir Winston replied. "But whenever I feel that way I always remember that, if instead of making a political speech I was being hanged, the crowd would be twice as big."

SPEEDING

Motorist stopped by traffic officer: "I was temporarily overcome by a wave of nostalgia. I thought the speed limit was seventy."

STORYTELLER

A good storyteller is a person who has a good memory and hopes other people haven't.

SUCCESS

Nothing recedes like success. WALTER WINCHELL

Success comes in cans; failure in can'ts.

The dictionary is the only place where success comes before work.

SUE

A first-grader slipped in the hall of the school and sprained his ankle. His teacher, hurrying to console him said, "Remember, Johnny, big boys don't cry."

"I'm not going to cry," snapped Johnny. "I'm going to sue."

SUICIDE

She: If I refuse to be your wife, will you really commit suicide?

He: That has been my usual procedure.

SUNBURN

I fell asleep on the beach and burned my stomach. You should see my pot roast!

SUNSHINE

All sunshine makes a desert.

SURPRISE

I was so surprised at my birth, I couldn't speak for a year and a half.

SWEATER

A garment worn by a child when his mother feels chilly.

SWELL

"I can't get into my shoes."

"What's the matter—did your feet swell, too?"

T is for Tomfoolery, Tremendous, Tickled

TACT

Tact is the ability to close one's mouth before someone else wants to do it.

TALK

Talk is cheap because the supply is greater than the demand.

Some people have the gift of compressing the largest amount of words into the smallest amount of thought. WINSTON CHURCHILL.

TEACHER

Teacher: A fool can ask more questions than a wise man can answer.

Student: No wonder so many of us flunk our exams.

TEETH

There are three basic rules for having good teeth:
1. Brush them twice a day.
2. See your dentist twice a year.
3. Keep your nose out of other people's business.

TELEVISION

Know what TV is? The place where little old movies go when they're bad.

The trouble with TV is that we sit so much watching the 21-inch screen we develop a 50-inch bottom.

TEMPTATION

When you flee temptation, be sure you don't leave a forwarding address.

Do we ever have a temptation without previous preparation?

Some temptations come to the industrious, but all temptations attack the idle. CHARLES HADDON SPURGEON

TEXAN

A Texas rancher was visiting an Iowa farm. The Iowa farmer was justly proud of his two hundred acres of rich, productive land.

"Is this your whole farm?" the Texan asked. "Why, back in Texas I get in my car at five in the morning, and I drive and drive all day. At dusk I just reach the other end of my ranch."

The Iowa farmer thought a while and replied, "I used to have a car like that."

THUMB

"Waiter," exclaimed the angry diner, "you've got your thumb on my steak!"

"I'm sorry sir," the waiter replied, "but I didn't want it to fall on the floor again."

TICKET

Jim: My wife just got a ticket for speeding.
John: That's nothing! My wife is so bad the police gave her a season ticket.

TIGHTWAD

Sharon: Is your husband tight with money?

> *Esther:* Is he! Every time he takes a penny out of his pocket, Lincoln blinks at the light.

TIME

Time may be a great healer, but it's a lousy beautician.

Why is it that there is never enough time to do it right, but there is always enough time to do it over!
MARK TWAIN

People who have half an hour to spend usually spend it with someone who hasn't.

Maybe people who are always on time aren't doing it to be courteous and polite. Maybe they're just mean, vicious people whose ambition in life is to make the rest of us feel guilty for being late.

TIP

Did you ever stop to think that the tip you leave for a meal today would have paid the whole bill ten years ago?

TONGUE TWISTER

According to the *Guinness Book of World Records,* the toughest tongue-twister in the English language is this one: "The sixth sick sheik's sixth sheep's sick."

TOP THIS

> *Bill:* My dog swallowed a tapeworm and died by inches.
> *Bob:* That's nothing—my dog crawled up in my bed and died by the foot.
> *Ken:* I can beat that. I had a dog that went out of the house and died by the yard.

TREADS

There was once a wise man who loved a beautiful maiden, but she lived in a marsh where his car always got stuck. Besides, her father had a gun, so he never did get close enough to tell her of his passion. However, she had a more energetic suitor who purchased amphibious tires for his car and, when her father was asleep, speedily carried her off.

Moral: Treads rush in where wise men fear to fool.

TRIFLES

A small leak will sink a great ship. BENJAMIN FRANKLIN

For the want of a nail the shoe was lost,
For the want of a shoe the horse was lost,
For the want of a horse the rider was lost,
For the want of a rider the battle was lost,
For the want of a battle the kingdom was lost,
And all for the want of a horseshoe nail.
BENJAMIN FRANKLIN

TROUBLE

The only fellow whose troubles are all behind him is a school bus driver.

Supply officer: Does the new uniform fit you?
Recruit: The jacket isn't bad, sir, but the trousers are a little loose under the armpits.

TRUTH

Any story sounds true until someone tells the other side and sets the record straight. PROVERB 18:17

Error always rides the back of truth.

U is for Unpredictable, Utterly Absurd, Unbelievable

ULCERS

A sorely pressed newlywed husband tried valiantly to console his little bride, who sprawled, dissolved in tears, on the sofa. "Darling," he implored, "believe me, I never said you were a terrible cook. I merely pointed out that our garbage disposal has developed an ulcer."

Wife I: Does your husband have ulcers?
Wife II: No, but he's a carrier!

UNDERTAKER

Dave: Did you hear about the snake charmer who married an undertaker?
Rich: No, what happened?
Dave: They had towels marked "Hiss" and "Hearse."

V is for Very Funny

VACUUM CLEANER

Mother: Glen, the canary has disappeared.

Glen: That's funny. It was there a minute ago when I cleaned the cage with the vacuum cleaner.

VEGETABLES

A vegetable is a substance used to balance a child's plate while it's being carried to and from the table.

Hostess to dinner guests: "All the vegetables are from our garden. You're eating a $100-a-plate dinner."

VOWS

Vows made in storms are forgotten in calm. THOMAS FULLER

 **is for Wit, Whimsy, Wisecracks, Wacky**

WATER BED
Esther: Why did you get rid of your water bed?
Sharon: Bill and I were drifting apart.

WEAK
A man is never so weak as when some woman is telling him how strong he is.

WEIGHT
Husband: I just lost ten pounds!
Wife: Turn around—I think I found them.

WHALE
If fish is brain food, you had better eat a whale.

WHISPER
Mother: What did you learn in school today?
Son: How to whisper without moving my lips.

WORD
A good word is as easily said as a bad one.

WORK
My father taught me to work; he did not teach me to love it. ABRAHAM LINCOLN

If you tickle the earth with a hoe, she laughs with a harvest.

An empty stable stays clean—but there is no income from an empty stable. PROVERBS 14:4

The trouble with opportunity is that it always comes disguised as hard work.

WRITING

'Tis pleasant, sure, to see one's name in print;
A book's a book, although there's nothin' in't.
LORD BYRON

Y is for Yarn, Young at Heart

YAWN

My friend, have you heard of the town of Yawn, on the banks of the river Slow, where blooms the Waitawhile flower fair, where the Sometimerother scents the air, and the Softgoeasys grow?

It lies in the valley of Whatstheuse, in the province of Letherslide; that tired feeling is native there—it's the home of the listless Idon'tcare, where the Putitoffs abide.

The audience was swell. They were so polite they covered their mouths when they yawned. BOB HOPE

A lady was complaining to her husband about the ill manners of a friend who had just left. "If that woman yawned once while I was talking, she yawned ten times."

"Maybe she wasn't yawning, dear," replied the husband. "Perhaps she was trying to say something."

YOUTH

Youth is a wonderful thing; what a crime to waste it on children. GEORGE BERNARD SHAW

Youth is that period when a young boy knows everything but how to make a living.

 **is for Zany**

ZEAL

A certain nervous disorder afflicting the young and inexperienced.